No Carbs No Sugar

A Beginner's 5-Step Guide to Smart Grocery Shopping

copyright © 2025 Bruce Ackerberg

All rights reserved No part of this book may be reproduced, or stored in a retrieval system, or transmitted in any form or by any means, electronic, mechanical, photocopying, recording, or otherwise, without express written permission of the publisher.

Disclaimer

By reading this disclaimer, you are accepting the terms of the disclaimer in full. If you disagree with this disclaimer, please do not read the guide.

All of the content within this guide is provided for informational and educational purposes only, and should not be accepted as independent medical or other professional advice. The author is not a doctor, physician, nurse, mental health provider, or registered nutritionist/dietician. Therefore, using and reading this guide does not establish any form of a physician-patient relationship.

Always consult with a physician or another qualified health provider with any issues or questions you might have regarding any sort of medical condition. Do not ever dis- regard any qualified professional medical advice or delay seeking that advice because of anything you have read in this guide. The information in this guide is not intended to be any sort of medical advice and should not be used in lieu of any medical advice by a licensed and qualified medical pro- fessional.

The information in this guide has been compiled from a variety of known sources. However, the author cannot attest to or guarantee the accuracy of each source and thus should not be held liable for any errors or omissions.

You acknowledge that the publisher of this guide will not be held liable for any loss or damage of any kind incurred as a result of this guide or the reliance on any information provided within this guide. You acknowledge and agree that you assume all risk and responsibility for any action you undertake in response to the information in this guide.

Using this guide does not guarantee any particular result (e.g., weight loss or a cure). By reading this guide, you acknowledge that there are no guarantees to any specific outcome or results you can expect.

All product names, diet plans, or names used in this guide are for identification purposes only and are the property of their respective owners. The use of these names does not imply endorsement. All other trademarks cited herein are the property of their respective owners.

Where applicable, this guide is not intended to be a substitute for the original work of this diet plan and is, at most, a supplement to the original work for this diet plan and never a direct substitute. This guide is a personal expression of the facts of that diet plan.

Where applicable, persons shown in the cover images are stock photography models and the publisher has obtained the rights to use the images through license agreements with third-party stock image companies.

Table of Contents

Introduction   7
Preparing for Your Shopping Trip   9
    Planning Ahead: The Importance of Meal Planning   9
    Making a Grocery List: Essentials vs. Optional Items   10
    Essential Items for a No-Carb, No-Sugar Diet   12
    Tips for Sticking to Diet Goals While Shopping   13
    Practical Additions to Your List   14
Mastering Food Labels   16
    How to Identify Hidden Sugars in Packaged Foods   16
    Common Names for Carbs and Sugars to Watch For   18
    Healthier Alternatives to Added Sugars   19
    Label-Reading Examples: What to Look For   20
    Practical Advice for Navigating Labels   21
The Ultimate No-Carb, No-Sugar Grocery List   23
    Protein Staples   23
    Vegetables   26
    Healthy Fats   28
    Snacks and Sweets   29
    Condiments and Seasonings   30
    Drinks   31
Where to Shop   32
    Navigating Grocery Stores   32
    Online Shopping for Convenience and Rare Finds   33
    Cost-Saving Strategies   34
    Advanced Tips for Smart Shopping   38
Budgeting for Your Diet   40
    Breaking Down Costs for Essentials   40
    Affordable Substitutes for Expensive Ingredients   42
    Balancing Quality with Affordability   43

Tracking and Planning Expenses 44
Leveraging Discounts and Bulk Purchases 45
Practical Tips for Long-Term Success 46
5 Step-by-Step to Shop for Your No-Carb, No-Sugar Diet **48**
Step 1: Start with Produce (Outer Aisles) 48
Step 2: Move to Protein Sources 52
Step 3: Stock Up on Healthy Fats 57
Step 4: Steer Clear of the Center Aisles 62
Step 5: Wrap Up with Frozen Foods When Needed 68
Dining Out and Eating Socially on a No-Carb, No-Sugar Diet 73
Conclusion **79**
FAQs **81**
References and Helpful Links **84**

Introduction

Shopping for a no-carb and no-sugar diet can feel like stepping into uncharted territory, filled with both challenges and opportunities. Grocery aisles brim with brightly packaged, processed foods that often hide unwanted ingredients in plain sight. This can make finding compliant options a tricky and time-consuming task for many.

This way of shopping requires a shift in perspective, changing how products are viewed and decisions are made. Understanding ingredient labels becomes essential, as does learning to identify hidden sugars and carbohydrates masquerading under unfamiliar names. It's not enough to rely on what looks healthy; careful attention to every small detail is key.

What makes this process so rewarding is the chance to explore an entirely fresh approach to food. While familiar staples might be off-limits, the opportunity arises to discover nutrient-dense, whole foods that bring variety to the table. Grocery trips turn into mini-adventures, uncovering items like almond flour, avocado oils, and low-carb vegetables that slip effortlessly into innovative recipes.

In this guide you will learn about the following;

- Preparing for Your Shopping Trip
- Mastering Food Labels
- The Ultimate No-Carb, No-Sugar Grocery List
- Where to Shop
- Budgeting for Your Diet
- 5 Step-by-Step Guide to Shop for Your No-Carb, No-Sugar Diet
- Dining Out and Eating Socially on a No-Carb, No-Sugar Diet

The aim is to take the guesswork out of every aisle, provide solutions for common hurdles, and spark inspiration for meals that bring excitement back into the kitchen. For anyone embarking on this lifestyle, it's all about making informed and deliberate choices—choices that empower and support long-term goals.

Preparing for Your Shopping Trip

A no-carb, no-sugar diet begins long before stepping foot in a grocery store; it starts with preparation. Building a solid plan sets the tone for success while minimizing the overwhelm that often comes with transitioning to a new way of eating. From meal planning to grocery lists and shopping strategies, a well-prepared approach makes it easier to stay consistent and aligned with dietary goals.

Planning Ahead: The Importance of Meal Planning

Meal planning goes beyond deciding what to eat—it's a strategy for staying consistent with the no-carb, no-sugar diet while reducing stress and saving time. By planning meals for the week ahead, there's less risk of feeling unprepared or succumbing to last-minute temptations. Start by allocating time each weekend to map out breakfast, lunch, dinner, and snacks for the coming week.

Focus on building meals around no-carb and no-sugar essentials while including enough variety to keep things interesting. For example, Monday's dinner might feature grilled salmon with asparagus, while Wednesday's could involve a hearty bun-less burger served with cauliflower mash. Taking this approach ensures you meet your nutritional needs without repetitive meals leading to boredom.

Batch cooking is another tool for success. Prepare ingredients or full meals in advance, such as baking chicken thighs, roasting vegetables, or cooking ground beef to use in various recipes throughout the week. Having ready-to-eat options reduces the allure of fast food or processed meals when life gets hectic.

Making a Grocery List: Essentials vs. Optional Items

A thoughtful grocery list is your game plan for navigating trips to the store effectively and within the boundaries of your diet. Categorize the list into essential and optional items to ensure your primary nutritional needs are covered while allowing some room for flexibility and creativity.

Essentials

These items form the foundation of your no-carb, no-sugar diet and should make up the majority of your purchases.

- *Fresh Vegetables:* Focus on nutrient-rich, low-carb options. Examples include spinach, kale, broccoli, cauliflower, cucumber, zucchini, bell peppers, and celery.

- ***High-Quality Proteins:*** Include grass-fed beef, free-range chicken or turkey, wild-caught fish (like salmon, tuna, or mackerel), and eggs.
- ***Healthy Fats:*** Stock up on avocados, olive oil, coconut oil, nuts (almonds, walnuts), and seeds (chia, flaxseed).
- ***Pantry Staples:*** Opt for ingredients like unsweetened almond milk, bone broth, almond flour, coconut flour, and canned fish like tuna or salmon.

Optional Items

Optional items can enhance your meals but aren't necessities for your weekly plan.

- ***Specialty Vegetables:*** Experiment with spaghetti squash for making low-carb "pasta," or stock up on cauliflower rice as a base for stir-fries.
- ***Snack Options:*** Sugar-free beef jerky, cheese sticks and dark chocolate (70% cacao or higher) are great ways to satisfy cravings within dietary goals.
- ***Seasonings and Condiments:*** Keep meals exciting by using coconut aminos, sugar-free hot sauces, or nutritional yeast for added flavor.

Organizing the list by grocery store sections can help streamline your shopping. For example, group all fresh produce together, followed by proteins and pantry staples. This method reduces time spent wandering the aisles and the temptation to deviate from your plan.

Essential Items for a No-Carb, No-Sugar Diet

Having go-to items at home will make sticking to your new lifestyle easier. Here's a detailed breakdown of essentials by category for a no-carb, no-sugar-friendly kitchen.

Fresh Vegetables

- Leafy greens like kale, spinach, and arugula (great for salads and sides)
- Cruciferous vegetables such as cauliflower, broccoli, and Brussels sprouts
- Low-carb alternatives like zucchini (perfect for noodles), spaghetti squash, or green beans

High-Quality Proteins

- Ground turkey or lean cuts of beef
- Wild-caught seafood like cod, shrimp, or scallops
- Eggs or egg whites for breakfast recipes and snacks

Healthy Fats

- Small avocados for snacking or adding to salads
- Mixed nuts (unsalted) and seeds for quick energy boosts
- Olive oil and avocado oil for cooking

Pantry Staples

- Low-sodium bone broth for soups or sipping
- Unsweetened coconut milk as a dairy alternative for coffee or smoothies

Snacking Options
- Nitrate-free beef or turkey jerky
- Cheese sticks or pre-portioned cheeses like cheddar or gouda

Tips for Sticking to Diet Goals While Shopping

Grocery stores are filled with temptations, but sticking to your diet goals is achievable with the right strategies in place.

1. *Eat Before You Shop:* Always shop on a full stomach. Hunger can lead to impulsive buys that don't align with diet goals.
2. *Stick to the Perimeter:* Focus on the outer aisles of the store where fresh produce, proteins, and dairy products are stocked. The interior aisles often house processed, sugary, or high-carb foods.
3. *Learn to Read Labels:* Many products hide sugars and carbs in ingredients like "maltodextrin," "evaporated cane juice," or "corn syrup solids." Be vigilant and check for hidden additives.
4. *Shop with Purpose:* Set a clear intention before walking in. Whether it's sticking to the list, exploring quality cuts of meat, or finding fresh leafy greens, having a purpose helps you stay focused.
5. *Visualize Your Goal:* Remind yourself how today's choices align with your long-term health goals. Each

decision in the store contributes to your greater commitment.

Practical Additions to Your List

Adding variety to your meals can help prevent monotony. Here are some practical additions for more creative and flexible meals.

- *Vegetable Alternatives:* Opt for riced cauliflower or spiralized zucchini for innovative, healthy sides.
- *Specialty Condiments:* Add sugar-free salad dressings, hot sauces, or soy replacement sauces like coconut aminos to elevate your recipes.
- *Savory Snacks:* Seaweed snacks, roasted nuts, or crab sticks can be enjoyable alternatives.

Preparation is the secret to thriving on a no-carb, no-sugar lifestyle. By planning meals, making mindful shopping lists, and using smart in-store strategies, every trip to the store becomes a confident step toward long-term health goals. Put thought into your shopping routine, and you're not just stocking up on food—you're investing in your future well-being.

Mastering Food Labels

Understanding how to read food labels can feel like unlocking a secret code, especially when following a no-carb, no-sugar diet. The challenge lies in identifying hidden sugars and carbs cleverly disguised within processed foods. With a bit of knowledge and practice, anyone can become more confident in deciphering labels and making better choices.

How to Identify Hidden Sugars in Packaged Foods

Sugar often sneaks into packaged foods under innocent-sounding names. While a product might not explicitly list "sugar," it could still contain sweeteners like honey or agave. Manufacturers also use unfamiliar terms to mask sugars, making label reading critical for staying on track.

Focus on three areas when analyzing a product's nutrition label:

1. **Ingredients List:**

    The ingredients are listed in descending order by weight. If sugar or its aliases appear near the top, that product likely has a high sugar content. Pay close attention to words like "syrup," "nectar," or anything ending in "-ose" (e.g., glucose, fructose). Even items branded as "low-fat" often compensate by boosting sugar content for taste.

2. **Total Carbohydrates:**

This section of the nutrition label reflects all carbs in the product, including naturally occurring ones. Look at "Added Sugars" specifically, as these are additional sweeteners that offer no nutritional benefit. Avoid products with a high percentage of added sugars.

3. **Marketing Claims:**

Beware of misleading claims like "natural," "organic," or "no refined sugar." These can still indicate substantial added sugar in forms like honey, molasses, or coconut sugar. Even "sugar-free" items sometimes use carbohydrate-based substitutes that impact blood sugar levels.

Here's a handy list of sugar aliases to memorize and avoid:

- High-fructose corn syrup
- Cane juice or cane sugar
- Dextrose
- Maltodextrin
- Brown rice syrup

- Molasses
- Coconut sugar
- Agave nectar
- Barley malt
- Evaporated cane juice

By mastering this terminology, it becomes easier to spot and bypass unwanted sugars hiding in processed or packaged items.

Common Names for Carbs and Sugars to Watch For

Added sugars and carbs disguise themselves under wholesome-sounding names, creating confusion for shoppers. Be on the lookout for ingredients like "malt syrup" or "fruit juice concentrate," especially in products marketed as health foods. Even supposedly better options, such as "organic cane sugar" or "maple syrup," can be just as harmful to your goals. Recognizing these varying names ensures you stick to your diet plan.

Examples of hidden carbs and sugars include:

- Maltose
- Lactose
- Sorbitol
- Rice syrup
- Fruit puree or juice concentrate

- Honey (often perceived as healthier but still adds sugar)

When in doubt, opt for whole, unprocessed foods where the ingredients are simple and straightforward.

Healthier Alternatives to Added Sugars

Craving something sweet is natural, but managing these cravings on a no-carb, no-sugar diet requires the right substitutes. Many natural or low-carb options can provide sweetness without compromising your goals. For example, fruit like berries or a sprinkle of cinnamon can enhance flavor without the added sugar impact.

Here's a more detailed look at substitutes for added sugars in recipes or snacks:

- *Stevia:* A natural, plant-based sweetener with zero calories that works well in beverages or baked goods.
- *Monk Fruit Sweetener:* Another zero-calorie alternative with a taste similar to sugar, ideal for cooking and baking.
- *Unsweetened Applesauce (in moderation):* Perfect for replacing sugar in savory dishes or desserts.
- *Pureed Dates:* Packed with natural sweetness, dates work in small quantities for desserts but should be used sparingly due to their carb content.

- ***Spices like Cinnamon or Nutmeg:*** These provide a sweet flavor profile and pair perfectly with hot drinks or roasted vegetables.
- ***Vanilla Extract or Almond Extract:*** A small amount can enhance sweetness and richness in recipes.

Substituting processed sugars with these alternatives not only keeps you within the boundaries of your diet but can also help you explore new flavors and textures in your meals.

Label-Reading Examples: What to Look For

Learning how to read labels can make a big difference when sticking to a no-carb, no-sugar diet. Here are some simple examples to help you compare products and make smarter choices.

1. ***Peanut Butter:*** Take two jars of peanut butter. The first one has just two ingredients—peanuts and salt. The second one lists sugar, molasses, or hydrogenated oils in the ingredients. Which one is better? It's the first jar! Always opt for products with fewer and straightforward ingredients when possible.
2. ***Granola Bars:*** Picture two granola bars. The first one lists ingredients like "honey," "cane sugar," or "brown rice syrup" close to the top of the ingredients list. The second one uses ingredients like nuts, seeds, and coconut, without adding sugars. The second bar is a

better choice for a no-carb, no-sugar diet because it prioritizes whole foods without sneaky carbs or sugars.

3. ***Flavored Drinks:*** Even drinks that seem "healthy," like flavored almond milk or sports drinks, can hide sugars. Check the label carefully. If sugar, syrups, or any "-ose" words like glucose or fructose show up in the ingredients, chances are it's not compliant with your diet. Pick unsweetened or plain options instead.

<u>**Pro Tip:**</u> Always focus first on the ingredients list and then double-check the "Total Carbohydrates" and "Added Sugars" sections on the nutrition panel. Products with added sugars or a big carb count probably won't fit your goals.

By taking a few extra seconds to compare labels, you'll make healthier choices and feel more in control of your shopping decisions. The key is to look for simple, whole ingredients and avoid products that sneak in unnecessary carbs or sugars.

Practical Advice for Navigating Labels

1. **Stick to Fewer Ingredients:**

   The fewer the ingredients, the less likely it contains hidden additives. Focus on minimal and recognizable components.

2. **Practice Decoding Ingredients:**

   Take note of the sugars and carbs you frequently see on labels. The more familiar you become, the faster you'll be able to decide what's truly healthy.

3. **Set Standards:**

   Create a threshold for carb or sugar intake—if a product exceeds this, place it back on the shelf.

4. **Test Alternatives:**

   Finding compliant sweeteners or products that fit your dietary needs can take time. Don't hesitate to experiment with recommended replacements or new recipes.

Mastering food labels is more than understanding what's in your food—it's about empowering yourself to make choices that align with your health goals. With time and practice, reading labels will become second nature, ensuring that every product you select supports your no-carb, no-sugar lifestyle. Stay vigilant, experiment with alternatives, and enjoy the process of reshaping your approach to food.

The Ultimate No-Carb, No-Sugar Grocery List

Switching to a no-carb, no-sugar diet can feel intimidating at first, but with the right approach and some strategic grocery shopping, the process becomes manageable—and even exciting! Having a well-stocked fridge and pantry ensures you're always prepared to make a healthy, satisfying meal without reaching for carb-heavy or overly sweetened options. This chapter provides a comprehensive guide to help you choose the best ingredients to fit your new lifestyle.

Protein Staples

Meat, Poultry, and Seafood Options

Protein forms the bedrock of any no-carb, no-sugar diet, offering essential nutrients to fuel your body and keep you satisfied. High-quality, whole cuts of meat, poultry, and seafood should be your go-to choices.

What to Look For:

- ***Beef:*** Opt for cuts like sirloin, ribeye, brisket, or ground beef. Whenever possible, choose grass-fed beef, as it often contains higher levels of omega-3 fatty acids and is free of antibiotics and hormones.
- ***Poultry:*** Choose skinless chicken breasts, thighs, or drumsticks if you want a leaner option, or keep the skin on for added satiety and flavor. Pasture-raised chicken or turkey is ideal for higher-quality protein.
- ***Pork:*** Pork tenderloin, chops, or ground pork are great picks. Look for heritage breeds or pasture-raised pork for more flavor and better nutrition.
- ***Seafood:*** Wild-caught salmon, tuna, mackerel, shrimp, scallops, and cod are nutrient-dense options rich in protein and heart-healthy fats, especially omega-3s. Shellfish like crab and lobster also work well, adding variety to your meals.

Pro Tip: Avoid pre-marinated or pre-seasoned meats unless you're sure about the ingredients. Many marinades contain sugar, starches, or preservatives that don't fit within this dietary plan.

Meal Ideas:

- Grill a salmon fillet alongside a medley of non-starchy vegetables.
- Slow-cook pulled pork seasoned with keto-approved spices for a hearty meal.

- Toss shrimp and scallops in garlic butter for a quick, delicious dinner.

Eggs and Dairy

Eggs are not only a breakfast staple but also one of the most versatile and affordable sources of protein. When selecting eggs, look for pasture-raised or organic varieties, which tend to have higher nutrient content and better flavor.

For dairy, the goal is to focus on low-carb, unsweetened options.

Eggs:

Scramble them with veggies, poach them for a light lunch, or make hard-boiled eggs to take on the go. They're a powerhouse of nutrients like choline and vitamin D.

Low- or No-Carb Dairy:

- *Hard Cheeses:* Cheddar, gouda, and parmesan are keto-friendly options for snacking or cooking.
- *Greek Yogurt:* Choose unsweetened, full-fat varieties, and sweeten with stevia or a handful of berries if desired. Some brands even provide a higher protein count, making them ideal as a base for dips or toppings.
- *Heavy Cream and Cream Cheese:* These add richness to recipes, from creamy soups to indulgent keto desserts.

Pro Tip: Even in dairy, hidden sugars can lurk in flavored or "low-fat" products. Always check the labels carefully!

Meal Ideas:

- Whisk eggs with spinach and feta for an easy omelette.
- Top roasted veggies with shredded parmesan for added crunch and flavor.
- Prepare a creamy cheese sauce using heavy cream and cheddar for low-carb pasta alternatives like zoodles or spaghetti squash.

Vegetables

Non-Starchy Vegetables

When it comes to vegetables, focus on low-carb, nutrient-packed options that help you meet your dietary goals while adding texture and variety to meals.

Best Choices:

- *Leafy Greens:* Spinach, kale, and arugula are full of vitamins and minerals, perfect for salads or stir-fries.
- *Cruciferous Vegetables:* Broccoli, cauliflower, and Brussels sprouts are fiber-rich and make excellent side dishes.
- *Others to Include:* Zucchini (great for zoodles), asparagus, bell peppers, mushrooms, and cucumbers.

- ***Health Benefits:*** Non-starchy vegetables are rich in vitamins, antioxidants, and dietary fiber that support gut health, reduce inflammation, and keep you feeling full.

Pro Tip: To save time, prep and chop vegetables in advance so they're ready for cooking or snacking during the week.

Meal Ideas:

- Roast zucchini, eggplant, and red bell peppers with a drizzle of olive oil for a colorful side dish.
- Use lettuce leaves as a substitute for bread in sandwiches or wraps.
- Riced cauliflower can replace traditional rice in dishes like fried rice or stuffed peppers.

Frozen vs. Fresh Options

Fresh vegetables are wonderful, but frozen veggies might be your best friend for convenience and meal prep. They're often picked at peak ripeness and flash-frozen, preserving their nutrients.

What to Buy:

- Frozen spinach, broccoli, cauliflower rice, and green beans are staples you can use in a pinch.
- Avoid frozen vegetables with added sauces or seasonings, as they often include hidden carbs and preservatives.

Tips for Use:

Steam frozen vegetables as a quick side dish, or toss them into soups and casseroles. Keep a mix of fresh and frozen options in your kitchen to reduce food waste.

Healthy Fats

Oils, Butter, and Fatty Snacks

Healthy fats are vital in a no-carb, no-sugar diet because they keep you feeling full and help balance your blood sugar levels.

Best Fats for Cooking and Flavor:

- Oils: Extra virgin olive oil, coconut oil, ghee, and avocado oil are flavorful and versatile. Use them for sautéing or as a base for salad dressings.
- Butter: Grass-fed butter provides a delicious way to enhance flavors and add creamy richness to dishes.

High-Fat Snacks:

- Pork rinds are a crunchy and savory option. Look for clean ingredient labels without artificial flavors.
- Fat bombs—made with coconut oil, cream cheese, or nut butter—are an easy DIY treat.

Pro Tip: Rotate your fats to get a mix of different nutrients and flavors.

Nuts and Seeds (Low-Carb Varieties)

Nuts and seeds provide healthy fats, protein, and a satisfying crunch.

Top Picks:

- Nuts like macadamia, pecans, almonds, and walnuts.
- Seeds such as chia, flaxseeds, and hemp hearts.

Tips for Buying:

Choose raw or dry-roasted varieties without added sugars or oils. Pre-portion them into small containers to avoid overeating, as they can be calorie-dense.

Meal Ideas:

- Sprinkle seeds over your salad for crunch.
- Use almond or sunflower seed butter in fat bomb recipes.

Snacks and Sweets

Low-Carb, No-Sugar Alternatives

You can find plenty of snack options that fit this lifestyle. Sugar-free chocolates made with stevia or erythritol are great for satisfying a sweet tooth.

Go-to Snacks:

Cheese crisps, jerky (without added sugar), boiled eggs, or keto snacks like flaxseed crackers.

DIY Snack Ingredients

Making your own snacks can be fun and puts you in control of the ingredients.

Ideas:

- Make kale chips or zucchini chips in the oven.
- Blend almonds and stevia to create homemade energy balls.

Condiments and Seasonings

Approved Spices and Flavorings

Use single-ingredient spices and fresh herbs to add depth to your dishes. Avoid blends with sugar or starch.

Essential Pantry Items:

Garlic powder, onion powder, smoked paprika, and turmeric. Fresh herbs like basil and cilantro elevate the flavor of cooked and raw dishes.

Sauces Without Hidden Carbs

Choose condiments labeled "sugar-free" or "keto." Examples include hot sauce, mustard, and mayonnaise made with avocado oil.

Pro Tip: Familiarize yourself with hidden sugar terms like "dextrose" and "high-fructose corn syrup" to spot tricky labels.

Drinks

What's Safe to Drink

Water is the gold standard! Add lime, lemon, or cucumber for flavor. Unsweetened herbal teas and black coffee are also safe.

Low-Carb Beverage Options:

- Unsweetened almond or coconut milk.
- Drink mixes sweetened with stevia or monk fruit offer alternatives to sugary sports drinks.

With this guide, mastering your no-carb, no-sugar grocery list becomes second nature. These staples set you up for success, ensuring that every meal is satisfying, nutritious, and aligned with your goals.

Where to Shop

Adopting a no-carb, no-sugar lifestyle requires more than just understanding what to eat—it's also about knowing where to shop for the right ingredients while staying within your budget. Thankfully, with the growing popularity of keto and low-carb diets, grocery shopping has become much easier.

From big-name chains to online stores, there are plenty of options that cater to your dietary needs. Here's how to make the most of your shopping experiences while saving money and finding high-quality ingredients.

Navigating Grocery Stores

Many grocery stores now cater to specialized diets with dedicated sections featuring organic, gluten-free, and keto-friendly offerings. For no-carb, no-sugar items, prioritize health-food sections and natural product aisles. Stores like Whole Foods Market and Trader Joe's make it simple to locate low-carb staples, while larger retail giants like Walmart and Target combine affordability with a growing range of keto options.

Examples of Top Chains and Their Benefits:

- *Whole Foods Market:* Known for its premium selection, this store carries a wide variety of keto-friendly snacks, fresh produce, and high-quality oils.
- *Trader Joe's:* A great source for quirky, affordable items like pre-spiralized zucchini noodles, cauliflower rice, and everything bagel seasoning.
- *Walmart and Target:* These mega-chains offer incredible value, with items like almond flour, sugar-free beverages, and affordable meats readily available.
- *Aldi:* Famous for budget-friendly prices, Aldi offers health-conscious items like keto crackers, meats, and low-carb cheeses at a fraction of the cost.

Pro Tip: When in doubt, check grocery store apps or websites ahead of time. Many stores now list their inventory online, making it easy to search for keto-friendly items before you shop.

Online Shopping for Convenience and Rare Finds

For hard-to-find kitchen staples like almond flour, coconut oil, or alternative sweeteners, online stores can be a game-changer. Alongside convenience, many online platforms specialize in keto and health-focused products, opening access to ingredients that might not be available locally.

Examples of popular online platforms include:

- *Thrive Market:* Offers a curated selection of discounted keto-friendly items, from cooking oils to ready-made snacks. Membership includes exclusive deals and promotions.
- *Amazon:* A one-stop shop for quick delivery of essential items like low-carb ketchup, keto bread, or sugar-free coffee syrups.
- *Netrition:* Specializes in low-carb and sugar-free goods, with helpful filters to simplify your search. Ideal for specialty products that are hard to find elsewhere.

Pro Tip: Utilize tools like "subscribe and save" on Amazon or membership perks from Thrive Market to get additional discounts on items you use regularly.

Cost-Saving Strategies

Eating a no-carb, no-sugar diet doesn't have to break the bank. With a few smart choices and planning, you can stick to your budget while enjoying a wide array of delicious and nutritious foods.

Budgeting for a Low-Carb Lifestyle

1. *Start with a Weekly Plan:* Create a meal plan each week, focusing on affordable staples like eggs, ground beef, chicken thighs, canned tuna, and seasonal

vegetables. Meal prep eliminates waste and keeps spending under control.
2. ***Track Your Spending:*** Monitor how much you're spending on groceries each week. Apps like Mint or even a simple spreadsheet can help you identify areas where you can cut back.
3. ***Prioritize Versatile Staples:*** Invest in ingredients that can be used across multiple meals. For example, cauliflower can be riced, mashed, or roasted, while eggs can serve as breakfast, snacks, or the base for a frittata.

Bulk-Buying Tips for Long-Term Savings

Purchasing in bulk significantly reduces cost per serving, especially for pantry staples and proteins. Stores like Costco are perfect for stocking up on essentials you'll use regularly.

Items to Buy in Bulk:

- Nuts and seeds (almonds, walnuts, chia seeds).
- Cooking oils (olive oil, coconut oil).
- Frozen vegetables (spinach, green beans, cauliflower rice).
- Meats (chicken breasts, ground beef, pork chops).

Storage Tips:

- Invest in a chest freezer to store bulk meat or seafood. Divide portions into freezer-safe bags for convenient meal prep.

- Use airtight containers to keep bulk nuts and seeds fresh. A refrigerator or cool pantry extends their shelf life.
- Vacuum-sealing leftovers reduces waste and prevents freezer burn.

Pro Tip: Check for sales at bulk stores and sign up for membership cards to access exclusive savings. Costco, for instance, frequently rotates discounts on keto-friendly options like almond flour and sugar-free snacks.

Shopping Off-Season and Making Discounts Work for You

1. ***Shop Produce When It's Cheapest:*** Seasonal fruits and vegetables are typically more affordable and nutritious. During summer, prioritize items like zucchini, cucumbers, and bell peppers. For winter months, stock up on hearty options like cabbage, Brussels sprouts, and cauliflower.
2. ***Freeze Seasonal Deals:*** When certain vegetables go on sale, buy in bulk and freeze them for later. For example, blanch zucchini slices or bell peppers before freezing so they're ready for stir-fries or casseroles.
3. ***Use Discounts Strategically:*** Many stores mark down perishable produce, dairy, or meat as it approaches its expiration date. If you plan to use these items immediately or freeze them, you can snag great deals.

Pro Tip: Sign up for grocery store loyalty programs to receive exclusive coupons, discount codes, or notifications about sales. Apps like Ibotta even offer cashback on specific purchases.

Farmers' Markets and Local Finds

Shopping locally provides two big advantages—freshness and affordability. Often, farmers' markets sell low-carb produce like spinach, kale, and zucchini at lower prices than supermarkets. Plus, you're supporting local farmers!

How to Maximize Value from Farmers' Markets:

- Go later in the day, when vendors may lower prices to clear stock.
- Buy in larger quantities and preserve extras through freezing or fermenting.
- Ask vendors about their growing practices if you're looking for organic options.

Look into Community Supported Agriculture (CSA) programs in your area. CSAs often offer weekly or bi-weekly boxes of fresh produce at a fixed cost, which can lead to considerable savings if you cook frequently.

Advanced Tips for Smart Shopping

How to Avoid Temptation in the Store

Grocery stores are designed to encourage impulse purchases, especially in aisles stocked with processed snacks and sugary drinks. Here's how to stay on track:

1. ***Make a Detailed Shopping List:*** A list keeps you focused and minimizes browsing.
2. ***Eat Before You Shop:*** Shopping on an empty stomach often leads to unnecessary (and less nutritious) purchases.
3. ***Stick to the Outside Aisles:*** Most stores place fresh produce, meats, and other whole foods along the perimeter. Avoid spending too much time in the center aisles, where processed goods dominate.

Same Staples, Lower Cost

- ***Generic Brands vs. Name Brands:*** Many grocery stores offer generic versions of popular keto ingredients (e.g., almond flour, cheeses). Compare ingredient lists and save on nearly identical products.
- ***DIY Staples:*** Instead of purchasing pre-spiralized zucchini noodles or cauliflower rice, make your own with a spiralizer or food processor at home. Pre-cut options are convenient but typically cost more.

By combining these strategies, you'll not only stick to your no-carb, no-sugar diet, but you'll also build a sustainable system for shopping smarter, eating well, and saving money.

Remember, every shopping trip is an opportunity to make choices that align with your goals and create delicious, nutritious meals for yourself and your family. With careful preparation and a little creativity, your keto shopping experience will be as rewarding as your results.

Budgeting for Your Diet

Maintaining a no-carb, no-sugar diet doesn't have to break the bank. By focusing on smart shopping, affordable substitutes, and mindful planning, you can stick to your dietary goals while staying within budget. This chapter dives into practical strategies to manage costs effectively, ensuring a healthy and sustainable lifestyle that works for you.

Breaking Down Costs for Essentials

When it comes to managing your budget, it's helpful to have a clear understanding of the staples you'll use most often. Think of these essentials as the building blocks of your meals. Items like eggs, chicken, fresh vegetables, and cooking oils are versatile and nutrient-dense—not to mention relatively affordable if you shop strategically.

Here's a breakdown of estimated costs for common keto essentials to help you plan more effectively (prices may vary based on location, quality, and purchase method):

- Eggs (dozen): $2.50–$4.00
- Chicken breast (per pound): $3.00–$5.00

- Ground beef (80/20) (per pound): $4.00–$6.00
- Leafy greens (per bunch or bag): $2.00–$4.00
- Avocados (each): $0.75–$1.50
- Cauliflower (head): $2.50–$4.00
- Almond flour (per pound): $6.00–$10.00
- Coconut oil (16 oz): $5.00–$8.00
- Cheese (per pound): $4.00–$8.00
- Nuts and seeds (per pound): $6.00–$12.00

Tips for Managing Costs

1. *Track Your Expenses:* Keep a weekly or monthly record of your grocery spending to understand where the bulk of your budget is going. This allows you to identify areas where you're overspending and make adjustments.
2. *Use a Meal Plan:* Plan your meals around affordable staples and versatile ingredients that can be used in multiple dishes. For example, a whole roasted chicken can provide meat for dinner, lunch salads, and even soup stock.
3. *Shop the Perimeter:* Focus on fresh produce, meats, and dairy sections, typically located around the edges of the store. These areas often house the most budget-friendly, whole-food items.

Affordable Substitutes for Expensive Ingredients

Not every item on a no-carb, no-sugar diet needs to be premium-priced. Finding affordable substitutes is key to sticking to your budget without compromising on nutrition or flavor.

Budget-Friendly Ingredient Swaps

- *Almond Flour vs. Coconut Flour:* Almond flour is well-loved in low-carb baking, but it can be pricy. Opt for coconut flour instead—it's more affordable and requires less per recipe since it's highly absorbent.
- *Avocado Oil vs. Olive Oil:* Replace avocado oil with olive oil for cost savings. Olive oil is widely available and versatile, whether for cooking or dressings.
- *Fresh Vegetables vs. Frozen:* Frozen broccoli, cauliflower, and spinach often cost less than fresh varieties and have a longer shelf life without losing nutritional value.
- *Grass-Fed Beef vs. Conventional Beef:* If grass-fed beef isn't in the budget, purchase conventional beef cuts from a trusted source. You can also go for ground beef, which is typically more affordable than steak or higher-end cuts.

DIY Staples to Cut Costs

Make some specialty items at home to reduce costs. For example, instead of buying pre-spiralized zucchini noodles or pre-riced cauliflower, use inexpensive tools like a spiralizer or food processor. These simple DIY efforts can save money in the long run.

Balancing Quality with Affordability

While it's tempting to focus solely on the lowest prices, investing in higher-quality ingredients for certain staples can make a big difference in your overall diet and satisfaction. The key is to strike a balance, splurging where it matters most while keeping supplemental costs down.

When to Invest in Quality

- *Meat and Eggs:* Whenever possible, choose pasture-raised eggs, grass-fed beef, wild-caught seafood, or organic chicken. These options often have higher nutrient levels, better flavor, and fewer additives compared to their conventional counterparts.
- *Healthy Fats:* Quality fats like olive oil, butter, or ghee can elevate the taste of meals while offering superior health benefits.

Economical Options Without Sacrifices

- *Conventional Produce:* If organic vegetables are too expensive, don't hesitate to choose conventional

varieties. Washing them thoroughly removes most pesticide residue, making them a perfectly healthy option.
- *Frozen Proteins:* Many budget-friendly stores offer frozen wild-caught fish or chicken, which can save you money without sacrificing nutritional value.

Smart Compromises

Reserve your budget for high-quality proteins and fats, and pair these with more cost-effective items like frozen vegetables, dry spices, or store-brand cheeses. This way, you still enjoy nutrient-rich meals while keeping costs under control.

Tracking and Planning Expenses

A well-organized approach to budgeting is essential for staying on track with both your dietary and financial goals.

Effective Expense Tracking

1. *Use Apps:* Try budget-friendly apps like EveryDollar or YNAB (You Need a Budget) to set monthly grocery limits and track spending in real-time. Categorize expenses into staples (protein, vegetables, fats) vs. splurges (snacks, specialty items).
2. *Keep Receipts:* Reviewing your receipts helps identify your top expenses and adjust future shopping habits. Highlight high-cost items and consider whether you can swap them for cheaper alternatives.

Plan Shopping Trips Ahead

- Check grocery store flyers or apps for weekly deals before heading out. Build meals around sale items like marked-down meats, bulk vegetables, or discounted oils.
- Stick to your shopping list to avoid impulse buys and unnecessary splurges.
- Avoid shopping on an empty stomach to reduce temptation for high-carb or sugar-laden items.

Leveraging Discounts and Bulk Purchases

Certain strategies can help you take advantage of discounts and bulk offers while avoiding waste.

1. *Stock Up During Sales:* Watch for discounts on ingredients you use regularly, such as olive oil, almond flour, or frozen meats, and buy in bulk when prices drop.
2. *Share Costs:* Split bulk purchases with friends or family to lower upfront expenses while still enjoying the savings.
3. *Portion and Freeze:* Freeze meats, cheeses, or vegetables in meal-sized portions to ensure they don't go to waste. For example, separate chicken breasts into individual freezer bags so you only defrost what you need.

Pro Tip: Use discount grocery apps like Ibotta or Fetch Rewards to claim cashback on eligible items or accumulate points for future savings.

Practical Tips for Long-Term Success

Sticking to a no-carb, no-sugar diet on a budget requires more than just a one-time strategy. Here are actionable tips to maintain financial balance over the long term:

1. *Meal Prepping Saves Dollars:* Cook several meals at once to save on time, energy, and food costs. For example, a single roast chicken can turn into roasted thighs for dinner, chicken salad for lunch, and broth for soups.
2. *Seasonal Menus Save Money:* Build meals around what's in season. For instance, focus on zucchini and tomatoes in summer, and swap to winter vegetables like spaghetti squash and Brussels sprouts when colder months hit.
3. *Find Freezer-Friendly Recipes:* Soups, casseroles, and stir-fries are budget-friendly, easy to make in large batches, and freeze well for future meals.

By combining smart planning and affordability-focused strategies, you'll be able to sustain your no-carb, no-sugar diet without putting a strain on your wallet. Remember, it's not about spending more but about spending smarter to create a lifestyle that is both healthy and financially sustainable.

5 Step-by-Step to Shop for Your No-Carb, No-Sugar Diet

Navigating a grocery store while sticking to your no-carb, no-sugar goals doesn't have to be overwhelming. With a focused approach, you can avoid temptations and leave with exactly what you need to support your lifestyle. Here's a simple step-by-step game plan to guide you through your shopping trip.

Step 1: Start with Produce (Outer Aisles)

When following a no-carb, no-sugar diet, the produce section is where you'll begin building the foundation of your meals. This area is often located around the store's perimeter, providing a wide array of fresh, nutrient-dense vegetables essential for your lifestyle. Here's how to maximize your produce selections and ensure you're choosing the best options for your health and budget.

Focus on Non-Starchy Vegetables

Non-starchy vegetables should make up the majority of your cart, as they deliver vitamins, minerals, antioxidants, and fiber without contributing to unwanted carbs or sugars. Some of the best choices include:

- *Leafy Greens:* Spinach, kale, arugula, chard, and romaine. These are highly versatile and can be used in salads, smoothies, or as a base for meals like lettuce wraps.
- *Cruciferous Vegetables:* Broccoli, cauliflower, cabbage, and Brussels sprouts. These are excellent for roasting, steaming, or even turning into low-carb alternatives like cauliflower rice or cauliflower mash.
- *Low-Carb Options:* Zucchini, cucumbers, green beans, asparagus, celery, and bell peppers. These add variety and crunch to meals without straying from your dietary goals.

Tips for Choosing the Freshest Produce

Selecting high-quality vegetables ensures your meals are not only nutritious but also taste their best. Follow these tips to make the most of your shopping trip:

- *Look for Vibrant Colors:* Bright greens, deep purples, and crisp whites often indicate freshness and high nutrient content. Avoid produce that looks wilted, bruised, or has blemishes.
- *Check for Firmness:* Vegetables like cucumbers, zucchini, and peppers should feel firm to the touch,

while leafy greens should appear crisp and free of yellowing edges.
- ***Inspect the Stems and Ends:*** For vegetables like broccoli or asparagus, vibrant and moist cuts at the stems indicate freshness, while drying or discoloration suggests they've been sitting out for a while.
- ***Smell Test:*** For herbs and leafy greens, a clean, fragrant aroma confirms freshness. Strong or unpleasant odors may signal spoilage.

Take Advantage of Seasonal Availability

Seasonal produce is not only fresher but often more affordable and flavorful. Buying vegetables at their peak season also supports local farmers and reduces the environmental impact of long-distance shipping. Here are some seasonal examples to guide your choices:

- ***Spring:*** Asparagus, spinach, radishes, and artichokes. These make for light and refreshing dishes like salads or quick sautés.
- ***Summer:*** Zucchini, cucumbers, bell peppers, and eggplant. Perfect for grilling, roasting, or zoodle dishes.
- ***Fall:*** Cauliflower, Brussels sprouts, kale, and cabbage. Great for soups, casseroles, and roasted side dishes.
- ***Winter:*** Broccoli, celery, collard greens, and leeks. These are hearty options for warm winter meals like stews or stir-fries.

Pro Tips to Maximize Your Produce Use

- *Shop Local:* Whenever possible, visit farmers' markets or local co-ops to find fresh, organic produce. Ask vendors about their growing practices to ensure you're getting pesticide-free or low-spray options.
- *Go for Bulk in Durable Veggies:* Vegetables like cabbage, celery, and kale last longer than delicate greens, making them great options for bulk-buying while reducing waste.
- *Freeze Extras:* If you find a good deal on seasonal produce, consider freezing extras. Veggies like spinach, broccoli, and cauliflower can be blanched and frozen to use later in soups, stir-fries, or baked meals.
- *Experiment with Cooking Methods:* To avoid monotony, try different methods like grilling, steaming, roasting, or air-frying. For example, roasted cauliflower tossed in olive oil or air-fried zucchini crisps are delicious, keto-friendly snacks.

By starting your grocery trip in the produce section and focusing on non-starchy, nutrient-dense vegetables, you'll build a solid base for your no-carb, no-sugar diet. Plan your meals around these fresh ingredients, and you'll always have something healthy and satisfying to enjoy while staying aligned with your health goals.

Step 2: Move to Protein Sources

Protein is a key component of a no-carb, no-sugar diet and plays a crucial role in keeping you energized, satiated, and maintaining muscle health. High-quality protein sources should be the next stop after gathering your produce.

Found along the store's perimeter, meats, poultry, seafood, and eggs are versatile, nutrient-dense options that can be used as the foundation for many delicious meals. Below, we'll break down how to select the best protein sources, their benefits, and tips for incorporating them into your weekly meal plan.

Select High-Quality Protein Sources

1. Meats
    - *Beef:* Look for cuts like sirloin, ground beef (80/20 ratio for flavor), ribeye, or brisket. Grass-fed beef is ideal for its higher levels of omega-3 fatty acids and lower traces of antibiotics or hormones.
    - *Pork:* Versatile and flavorful options include pork chops, tenderloin, or ground pork, all of which are great for grilling, roasting, or pan-searing. Select fresh cuts rather than pre-seasoned to avoid hidden sugars or starches.
    - *Lamb:* Cuts such as lamb chops or ground lamb are fatty and flavorful, making them perfect for a no-carb diet.

2. Poultry
    - ***Chicken:*** Choose skinless chicken breasts, thighs, drumsticks, or even a whole chicken for meal prep versatility. Opt for organic or pasture-raised chicken when possible.
    - ***Turkey:*** Ground turkey or turkey breasts are excellent lean options, especially for burgers, soups, or stir-fries.
    - ***Game Meats:*** If you're looking for variety, consider duck, quail, or other game meats—these are naturally rich in protein and often have higher fat content compared to chicken.
3. Seafood
    - ***Fatty Fish:*** Wild-caught salmon, mackerel, and trout are loaded with healthy omega-3 fatty acids, which are great for heart and brain health.
    - ***Shellfish:*** Shrimp, scallops, crab, and lobster add variety and texture to your meals without added carbs or sugar.
    - ***White Fish:*** Cod, halibut, or sole are leaner options with subtle flavors that work well in a variety of dishes.
    - ***Canned Seafood:*** Canned tuna, salmon, or sardines are affordable and shelf-stable options that can be thrown into salads or eaten as a quick snack.
4. Eggs

Eggs are an affordable, versatile protein option. Opt for pasture-raised or organic varieties whenever possible for richer flavor and higher nutrient content. Eggs can be used in breakfast dishes, baked goods, or even as a protein boost in salads.

Benefits of Different Protein Types

- *Beef and Lamb:* Packed with iron, zinc, and B vitamins, these meats support energy and immune function. The natural fats found in beef and lamb are ideal for staying satiated on a no-carb diet.
- *Poultry:* A leaner protein source that is easy to prepare, poultry offers flexibility and works across cuisines, whether you're grilling, baking, or stir-frying.
- *Seafood:* Loaded with omega-3s and essential minerals like selenium, seafood is both light and satisfying. It adds diversity to your meal plan.
- *Eggs:* A powerhouse of protein, healthy fats, and essential nutrients like choline, eggs are a convenient, quick option for any meal.

Tips for Choosing Quality Proteins

1. *Check for Freshness:* Always look for bright, red meat rather than dull or grayish tones. For fish, bright, clear eyes and a clean ocean smell signal freshness.

2. ***Look for Marbling in Beef:*** Fat marbling (the white streaks in beef) indicates tenderness and flavor, making it an excellent choice for a rich, satisfying meal.
3. ***Buy Whole Chickens:*** A whole chicken is often more affordable per pound than individual cuts and can be used across multiple meals.
4. ***Opt for Wild-Caught Seafood:*** Whenever your budget allows, wild-caught options are preferable over farmed fish for their superior nutrient profile and flavor.
5. ***Inspect Labels:*** Avoid meats or seafood that have been pre-marinated or cured unless labeled as "sugar-free" or "keto-friendly." Many marinades and cures include sugar or starch.

Practical Meal Prep Tips for Proteins

1. ***Batch Cook:*** Grill a large portion of chicken breasts or thighs at the beginning of the week and store them in the fridge for use in meals or salads.
2. ***Utilize a Slow Cooker:*** Make shredded beef, pulled pork, or chicken drumsticks in a slow cooker for hands-off cooking. Add keto-friendly spices or herbs for variety.
3. ***Portion and Freeze:*** Buy meats in bulk to save money, then divide them into meal-sized portions before freezing. This preserves freshness and simplifies prep on busy days.

4. ***Use Bone Broth:*** Save chicken or beef bones to make homemade bone broth. It's perfect for soups, braising vegetables, or sipping as a warm, nutrient-rich drink.
5. ***Marinate Overnight:*** Prepare proteins like chicken or fish the night before by marinating in olive oil, garlic, and keto-approved spices like paprika or oregano for an extra boost of flavor.

Pro Tips for Staying on Budget with Proteins

- ***Shop Sales:*** Look for weekly discounts on meat or seafood. Stores often mark down proteins approaching their "sell-by" date—freeze them immediately to extend shelf life.
- ***Consider Frozen Options:*** Frozen fish or chicken can be more affordable and just as nutritious as fresh options.
- ***Explore Off-Cuts:*** Cuts like chicken thighs, pork shoulder, or stew meat are less expensive but full of flavor.
- ***Buy Local:*** Check out farmers' markets or butcher shops for seasonal deals on fresh, high-quality meat.

By focusing on high-quality proteins and planning your meals around them, you'll ensure that your no-carb, no-sugar diet stays satisfying, nutrient-rich, and tailored to your health goals. Remember to always pair proteins with nutrient-dense vegetables and healthy fats for a balanced plate every time!

Step 3: Stock Up on Healthy Fats

Healthy fats are critical to a no-carb, no-sugar diet as they provide energy, support brain function, maintain satiety, and add richness and flavor to meals. Step three takes you to the sections of the store where you can find high-quality oils, nuts, seeds, and dairy products. These versatile ingredients will become foundational building blocks for your recipes. Here's how to choose the best options and maximize their potential in your kitchen.

Why Healthy Fats Are Essential

Unlike carbs or sugar, fats are an efficient source of energy that fuel your body without spiking blood sugar levels. Including a variety of fats in your diet ensures you're able to meet your nutritional needs while keeping meals satisfying and delicious. They also enhance the absorption of fat-soluble vitamins like A, D, E, and K found in your vegetables and proteins.

Choosing the Best Healthy Fats

1. Cooking Oils
    - *Olive Oil:* Extra virgin olive oil is rich in monounsaturated fats and antioxidants. It's ideal for salad dressings or drizzling over roasted veggies but should be used on low to medium heat when cooking to maintain its nutrients.
    - *Coconut Oil:* Known for its rich flavor and high smoke point, this oil is perfect for sautéing,

baking, and even blending into coffee for a creamy texture. Its medium-chain triglycerides (MCTs) provide a quick energy boost.
- ***Avocado Oil:*** With a neutral flavor and high smoke point, avocado oil is perfect for frying, roasting, and drizzling over salads. It's packed with heart-healthy monounsaturated fats.
- ***Ghee (Clarified Butter):*** Because ghee is free of milk solids, it's suitable for high-heat cooking and adds a rich, nutty flavor to dishes. Use it for stir-fries or to baste proteins.

2. Nuts and Seeds
   - ***Best Picks:*** Almonds, walnuts, macadamia nuts, and pecans are keto-friendly options loaded with healthy fats, fiber, and plant-based protein. For seeds, chia, flaxseed, sunflower, and hemp seeds are great choices for fiber and omega-3s.
   - ***What to Avoid:*** Steer clear of nuts and seeds coated in sugary or flavored coatings. Opt instead for raw or dry-roasted versions to keep your snack choices clean.

3. Dairy Products
   - ***Cheese:*** Hard cheeses like parmesan, cheddar, gouda, and gruyère are low in carbs and high in fat, making them perfect for snacking or melting over dishes.

- ***Full-Fat Yogurt or Greek Yogurt:*** Look for unsweetened versions with no added sugars. These can be used in savory dips or paired with berries for a light dessert.
- ***Heavy Cream:*** A great addition to coffee, soups, or desserts, it adds creaminess without adding sugar.
- ***Butter:*** Grass-fed butter provides flavor while delivering omega-3s and vitamins like K2. It's a staple for pan-frying or baking.

4. Pantry Staples
    - ***Nut Butters:*** Almond, macadamia, or sunflower seed butter are excellent spreads or additions to smoothies. Choose natural options with no added sugar or oils.
    - ***Coconut Milk or Coconut Cream:*** These are great for curries or as a base for creamy soups and desserts. Always check for unsweetened varieties.
5. Packaged Snacks

While you're in the store, check for keto-friendly snack options like pork rinds, roasted seaweed snacks, or pre-portioned nut and seed packs. These make easy on-the-go options for busy days.

Benefits of Different Types of Healthy Fats

Each type of fat offers unique nutritional benefits, so aim to include a variety.

- *Monounsaturated Fats (e.g., olive oil, avocados):* Help reduce inflammation and improve heart health.
- *Polyunsaturated Fats (e.g., walnuts, chia seeds):* Provide omega-3 fatty acids that promote brain and joint health.
- *Saturated Fats (e.g., butter, coconut oil):* Offer stability for cooking at higher heat and long-lasting energy.

How to Incorporate Healthy Fats Into Your Diet

- *Breakfast:* Fry eggs in butter, drizzle olive oil over an avocado half, or prepare a smoothie with unsweetened coconut milk and a spoonful of almond butter.
- *Lunch:* Toss a green salad with olive oil and lemon juice, and top it with grilled chicken, avocado slices, and hemp seeds for crunch.
- *Snacks:* Have a handful of macadamia nuts or pecans with a slice of cheese. Or use celery sticks to scoop up homemade guacamole.
- *Dinner:* Roast asparagus in avocado oil or sauté mushrooms with butter and garlic. Pair these with a fatty fish like salmon for a complete, hearty meal.

- *Desserts:* Use heavy cream to whip up a no-sugar-added mousse or pair unsweetened coconut cream with berries as a light treat.

Meal Prep and Planning Tips for Healthy Fats

1. ***Stock Your Pantry:*** Keep coconut oil, olive oil, and avocado oil in stock for everyday cooking. Store nuts and seeds in airtight containers to maintain freshness.
2. ***Divide Portions:*** Pre-portion nuts into small containers or resealable bags to prevent overeating and make snacks grab-and-go friendly.
3. ***Use Fats for Cooking and Finishing:*** Start dishes with fats like butter or ghee for sautéing and finish with a drizzle of olive oil for flavor.
4. ***Make Your Own Sauces:*** Combine olive oil with herbs or garlic to make an easy dressing or sauce. Coconut milk can be blended with spices for a creamy curry base.
5. ***Freeze Fats:*** Butters and oils like ghee can be frozen in small batches, ensuring you always have them on hand for recipes.

How to Spot Hidden Carbs in Fats

Even within this category, some products sneak in sugar or carbs, so always read the labels.

- ***Nut Butters:*** Watch out for brands with added sugars or oils like palm oil.

- ***Packaged Snacks:*** Check the ingredient list for starch-based coatings on seeds or nuts.
- ***Flavored Oils:*** Some infused oils can include additives or sweetening agents. Go for plain, unflavored options.

Pro Tips for Staying on a Budget

- ***Shop Bulk:*** Stores like Costco or Aldi often sell olive oil, nuts, and seeds in bulk quantities for significant savings.
- ***Generic Brands:*** Compare store-brand items, such as olive oil or butter, to premium brands. They often meet the same quality at a lower price.
- ***Watch for Sales:*** Stock up on ghee, coconut oil, and other items when they're on sale, as they have a long shelf life.

By focusing on healthy fats, you'll not only enjoy rich, satisfying meals but also set your body up for sustainable energy and improved overall health. These versatile ingredients are your allies in crafting flavorful, wholesome dishes aligned with your no-carb, no-sugar lifestyle!

Step 4: Steer Clear of the Center Aisles

While the perimeter of a grocery store is your go-to for fresh produce, proteins, and fats, you may occasionally need to venture into the center aisles for pantry staples. The challenge here lies in avoiding the sugary cereals, snack foods, and carb-heavy processed options that dominate these shelves. With a clear game plan and an eye for reading labels, you can make mindful choices to stock your pantry with items that support your no-carb, no-sugar lifestyle.

Why the Center Aisles Can Be a Trap

The majority of processed foods are found here, and these products are often packed with hidden sugars, preservatives, and refined carbs. Even seemingly "healthy" options like granola bars, flavored yogurts, or dried fruit often come with added sugars or starches disguised as natural ingredients. However, the center aisles do stock some essential diet-friendly pantry items—so the key is to shop smartly and stick to your list.

What to Look for in the Center Aisles

Here are some pantry staples you can grab while sticking to your diet plan.

1. Canned and Packaged Proteins
    - ***Canned Fish:*** Stock up on tuna, salmon, mackerel, or sardines. These are excellent for quick meals or snacks and are packed with healthy fats and protein. Choose options packed in water or olive oil and check for "no added sugar" on the label.
    - ***Shelf-Stable Meats:*** Look for high-quality jerky or meat sticks labeled sugar-free or keto-

friendly. These are great for portable protein on-the-go.

2. Pantry-Friendly Fats
    - ***Unsweetened Coconut Milk or Cream:*** These can be used for curries, soups, or dairy-free desserts. Read labels carefully to ensure no added sugars are included.
    - ***Nut or Seed Butters:*** Keep almond, macadamia, or sunflower seed butter on hand for snacking or adding to smoothies. Choose ones made with "just nuts" and steer clear of those containing sugar or hydrogenated oils.
3. Condiments and Flavor Enhancers
    - ***Coconut Aminos:*** A flavorful, low-carb alternative to soy sauce that works in stir-fries, marinades, or as a dipping sauce.
    - ***Mustard:*** Dijon, yellow, or stone-ground mustard are excellent low-carb condiments. Avoid honey mustard or variations that include sweeteners.
    - ***Sugar-Free Ketchup:*** Swap traditional ketchup with a keto-friendly, sugar-free option for a healthier topping or ingredient.
    - ***Vinegars:*** Stock up on apple cider vinegar, white vinegar, or balsamic vinegar (in small amounts) to add tangy notes to dressings or marinades.
4. Spices and Herbs

Dried spices and herb blends can completely transform your meals, offering variety and depth of flavor. Look for options without added fillers like starch or sugar. Common staples include garlic powder, paprika, turmeric, black pepper, cumin, oregano, and thyme.

5. Broths and Stocks

Unsweetened chicken, beef, or vegetable broth is an ideal base for soups and stews. Bone broth is another excellent choice for its high collagen content and robust flavor.

6. Snacks and Emergency Foods
   - ***Roasted or Raw Nuts and Seeds:*** Pre-portioned options can help control serving sizes. Be sure to avoid mixes with dried fruits or sugary coatings.
   - ***Pork Rinds:*** These are a great crunchy, zero-carb snack option. Look for plain or lightly salted varieties to avoid added sugars.
   - ***Seaweed Snacks:*** These provide a light, salty snack with no carbs. Choose unsweetened, unseasoned versions to avoid hidden ingredients.

How to Read Labels Like a Pro

Hidden sugars and carbs often lurk in unsuspecting products. Here's how to catch them before they sneak into your cart:

1. ***Check the Ingredient List:*** Look for words like "maltodextrin," "corn syrup," "dextrose," "fructose," or even "evaporated cane juice," which all signal added sugars.
2. ***Look for Total Carbs:*** Ideally, the total carbs listed on the label (minus fiber) should be as low as possible. Aim for items with 1-3 grams of net carbs per serving.
3. ***Watch Serving Sizes:*** Sneaky packaging can make an item appear low-carb, but the serving size may be unrealistically small (e.g., a tablespoon of a sauce or half a snack bar). Always pay attention to how much you're likely to eat versus what the label defines as a serving.
4. ***Compare Products:*** Look for similar items side-by-side and opt for the version with the fewest carbs, cleanest ingredient list, and no added sugars.

Practical Tips for Center Aisle Shopping

1. ***Stick to Your List:*** A detailed shopping list helps you avoid impulse buys and stay on track. List out exactly what you need for specific recipes or snacks, and stick to it.
2. ***Stay Focused:*** Resist the temptation to browse new or indulgent items in the snack or dessert aisles. If you do need a specific product from these sections, head straight to it with purpose.

3. **Shop Strategically:** Center aisles are where stores tend to place promotions on sugary snacks or tempting treats. Be mindful of "deals" that may steer you away from your no-carb, no-sugar goals.
4. **Prioritize Shelf-Stable Essentials:** Think ahead and stock up on items like canned fish, oils, or broths during sales. These items have a long shelf life and can reduce the need for frequent trips to the center aisles.
5. **Choose Bulk or Multipacks:** Nut butters, oils, and coconut milk are often cheaper per unit when bought in bulk, which can help you save money while staying stocked up.

Avoid Common Pitfalls

- *Pre-Made Sauces and Dressings:* These often contain sugar, cornstarch, or other carb-heavy thickeners. Make your own dressing with olive oil, vinegar, and spices instead.
- *"Low-Fat" or "Diet" Options:* These products frequently compensate for reduced fat content with added sugars.
- *"Natural" Claims:* Even products labeled as "all-natural" or "whole grain" can hide sugars, so always examine the ingredient list.

By carefully selecting pantry essentials and paying close attention to labels, you can venture into the center aisles without losing sight of your health goals. Discipline, preparation, and an unwavering focus on your list will ensure that the items you bring home fully align with your no-carb, no-sugar lifestyle. Steer clear of traps and shop with confidence!

Step 5: Wrap Up with Frozen Foods When Needed

The frozen food section can be your secret weapon for maintaining a no-carb, no-sugar lifestyle while keeping things convenient. Frozen produce and proteins are not only budget-friendly but also long-lasting, ensuring you always have wholesome ingredients on hand. This is especially helpful for busy weeks or when your fresh produce runs out. Here's how to make the most out of this section while staying in line with your diet goals.

Why Frozen Foods Are a Great Backup

Contrary to popular belief, frozen foods can often match or even surpass fresh foods in nutritional value because they're flash-frozen at peak ripeness. This means they retain key vitamins and minerals that can sometimes degrade in fresh produce during transport and storage. Additionally, frozen items give you flexibility—no need to worry about spoilage or the ticking clock of fresh ingredients.

Frozen foods also make meal prep faster and more efficient. With pre-chopped or pre-spiralized options like cauliflower rice or zucchini noodles, you can save time and reduce prep work without compromising on quality.

What to Look For in the Frozen Section

Vegetables

Non-starchy vegetables are staples of a no-carb, no-sugar diet, and the frozen aisle is packed with great options.

Go-To Picks:

- Broccoli Florets
- Spinach
- Green Beans
- Cauliflower (whole, florets, or riced)
- Asparagus Spears
- Brussel Sprouts
- Zucchini (spiralized or sliced)

What to Avoid: Stay away from vegetables with added sauces, breading, or seasoning packs. These often include hidden sugars, starches, or preservatives that don't align with your diet.

Fruits (Optional for Specific Plans)

If your diet allows for occasional fruits, frozen berries such as raspberries, blackberries, or strawberries are excellent choices. These are naturally low in sugar and can be added to smoothies or eaten in moderation with cream or coconut milk.

Proteins

While proteins are usually better from the fresh or refrigerated section, the frozen aisle can still offer high-quality options for convenience.

- Look for frozen shrimp, wild-caught salmon, cod, or other seafood options. They're easy to defrost and perfect for quick meals.
- Avoid pre-seasoned or breaded proteins, as these often contain sugar or starches.

Other Staples

- *Herbs:* Frozen basil, cilantro, or parsley are excellent to have on hand for adding bursts of fresh flavor without worrying about spoilage.
- *Cauliflower Crusts or Pizza Bases:* If you're in a pinch and craving a carb-free alternative, some frozen sections may carry cauliflower-based pizza crusts. Read the labels carefully to ensure there are no unnecessary additives.

How to Incorporate Frozen Foods Into Meals

1. *Quick Side Dishes:* Steam frozen broccoli, cauliflower, or green beans as a nutrient-packed side dish to complement proteins like grilled chicken or steak.
2. *Soups and Stews:* Toss frozen spinach or kale into soups during the last few minutes of cooking for a

hearty boost of greens. Frozen seafood like shrimp can also be added directly to boiling broth for a quick protein option.

3. *Stir-Fries:* Use a mix of frozen veggies like zucchini, bell peppers, and cauliflower rice as a base for a low-carb stir-fry. Pair with coconut aminos and your favorite protein for an easy one-pan dinner.
4. *Smoothies:* Blend frozen spinach or a handful of frozen berries with unsweetened almond milk and a spoonful of almond butter for a refreshing, filling drink.
5. *Casseroles:* Layer frozen cauliflower rice or zucchini with cooked proteins, cheese, and spices to create a comforting dish that's easy to bake and serves the whole family.

Tips for Buying and Storing Frozen Foods

1. *Stick to Plain, Unseasoned Options:* Products labeled "lightly seasoned" or "buttery" often contain hidden sugars or processed additives. Choosing plain options gives you full control over seasoning and flavors.
2. *Check for Quality Packaging:* Look for sturdy, well-sealed bags without clumps of ice inside, which could indicate thawing and refreezing has occurred.
3. *Buy in Bulk:* Frozen foods often come with discounts for buying larger packs. Stocking up during sales can reduce time spent shopping and cut down on costs.

4. ***Defrost Properly:*** For vegetables, steaming or microwaving while frozen works perfectly. For proteins, defrost in the fridge overnight to maintain texture and flavor.
5. ***Label and Organize:*** Keep your freezer clutter-free by labeling bags with purchase dates and organizing by category (e.g., vegetables, proteins, herbs). This helps avoid freezer burn and minimizes waste.

Avoiding Common Pitfalls

- ***Avoid Pre-Made Frozen Dinners:*** Many frozen meals, even those marketed as "healthy," sneak in carbs or sugars through sauces or fillers.
- ***Skip Sweetened Smoothie Mixes:*** These often include artificial sweeteners or sugary fruits that derail your low-carb lifestyle.
- ***Beware of Imitation Foods:*** Products like veggie tots or cauliflower nuggets may sound healthy but can be filled with carb-heavy additives like breadcrumbs or potato starch.

Pro Tips for Making the Most of Frozen Foods

- Take one day at the start of the week to prep meals that incorporate frozen veggies and proteins—this saves time during hectic weekdays. For instance, cook and portion out meals using frozen spinach or riced cauliflower as a base.

- Always have a few frozen "emergency" items on hand like shrimp or broccoli florets. These can help you whip up a no-carb, no-sugar meal in minutes, especially when fresh produce runs low.
- Use frozen herbs for enhancing flavors in sauces, marinades, or dressings—this saves effort from chopping and keeps your meals vibrant.

By wrapping up your shopping trip in the frozen food section, you add an extra layer of security to your meal plan. Stock your freezer with high-quality, nutrient-dense options, and you'll always have the tools on hand to create delicious, no-carb, no-sugar meals, even when life gets busy. Stay focused on plain, unseasoned choices, and turn convenience into a key part of your diet strategy!

Dining Out and Eating Socially on a No-Carb, No-Sugar Diet

Dining out or attending social gatherings while following a no-carb, no-sugar lifestyle doesn't have to be stressful or restrictive. With a little preparation and a confident approach, you can stick to your goals while still enjoying the experience. Whether you're navigating different cuisines or social expectations, these practical tips will help you stay on track.

General Strategies for Dining Out

1. ***Do Your Research:*** Check the restaurant's menu online beforehand if possible. Look for dishes that focus on proteins and vegetables, and identify options that can be easily customized to fit your diet.
2. ***Communicate Clearly:*** Don't be afraid to ask your server questions. For example:
   - "Is there sugar or starch in the sauce?"
   - "Can I have the vegetables steamed instead of sautéed in sauce?"
   - "Can I substitute extra greens or vegetables for the bread or fries?"

   Most restaurants are willing to accommodate dietary preferences if you ask politely.
3. ***Start with a Salad or Broth-Based Soup:*** Opt for simple starters like a green salad with olive oil and vinegar or a cup of unsweetened bone broth. These options keep you aligned with your diet while adding flavor to your meal.
4. ***Request Sauces and Dressings on the Side:*** Many sauces, dressings, and marinades contain hidden sugars or thickeners. By asking for them on the side, you can control how much you use—or skip them entirely.
5. ***Focus on Protein and Non-Starchy Veggies:*** Build your meal around grilled, roasted, or baked proteins like steak, chicken, or seafood, paired with non-starchy

vegetables such as spinach, asparagus, or broccoli. Avoid breaded, battered, or fried items.
6. ***Skip the Bread Basket and Desserts:*** When the bread basket or dessert menu comes around, politely decline or ask the staff to remove the temptation from the table. If social pressure is high, engage in conversation during dessert to take the focus off eating.
7. ***Drink Smartly:*** Stick to water, sparkling water, black coffee, or unsweetened tea instead of sugary beverages or cocktails. If you'd like an alcoholic drink, go for dry wine, champagne, or spirits like vodka or whisky—just skip the sugary mixers.

Navigating Different Cuisines

<u>Italian:</u>

- Look for grilled fish or chicken dishes with sides of vegetables.
- Skip the pasta and pizza. Instead, ask if the chef can substitute zucchini noodles (zoodles) or offer extra salad.

<u>Mexican:</u>

- Opt for fajitas without tortillas, and load up on grilled proteins, peppers, and guacamole.
- Avoid rice, beans, and chips, and ask for lettuce wraps instead of tortillas.

Asian:

- Sushi rolls are often out due to rice and sauces, but sashimi (just the fish) is an excellent choice.
- Choose stir-fried or grilled dishes like beef and broccoli, but confirm they aren't coated in sugary sauces or thickened with corn starch.
- Opt for coconut milk-based curries, ensuring no added sugar is used.

American Grill or Steakhouse:

- Stick with classic steak, grilled chicken, or salmon, paired with a side salad or steamed veggies.
- Avoid fries, mashed potatoes, or carb-heavy sides—most steakhouses happily offer alternative vegetable options.

Indian:

- Tandoori chicken, lamb kebabs, or grilled fish are great options.
- Choose dishes with cream or yogurt-based sauces, but verify there's no sugar added. Skip naan bread, rice, and lentils, and ask for extra sautéed or steamed vegetables.

Handling Social Gatherings

1. *Be Honest About Your Needs:* If you're attending a gathering with close friends or family, share your

dietary preferences in advance. Most hosts will be understanding and happy to accommodate you.

2. ***Offer to Bring a Dish:*** Bringing a no-carb, no-sugar dish to the party ensures at least one option fits your lifestyle. Consider making a big salad, veggie platter with a sugar-free dip, or a keto-friendly casserole.
3. ***Fill Up Before You Go:*** If you're unsure about the food options at a gathering, eat a satisfying meal before arriving. This will help you avoid cravings and prevent you from nibbling on foods that don't align with your diet.
4. ***Focus on the Social Aspect:*** When food is the main attraction at an event, it's easy to get caught up in what's on the table. Shift your focus to connecting with people, enjoying conversations, and being present.
5. ***Be Prepared for Questions or Comments:*** If others ask about your choices, keep your explanation simple and positive. You could say something like, "I feel my best when I avoid carbs and sugar," and then change the subject.
6. ***Stay Hydrated:*** Sip on water, sparkling water, or unsweetened beverages throughout the gathering to stay full and hydrated without adding calories.

Managing Portions

When dining out or eating socially, portion sizes can quickly become a challenge. Here's how to stay in control:

- Eat slowly, and listen to your hunger cues. Stop eating when you're satisfied, not stuffed.
- If dining at a restaurant, don't be afraid to ask for a to-go box and save half your meal for later.
- Avoid "family-style" servings at social events. Instead, serve yourself a single plate of food and stick to it.

By adopting these strategies, you can enjoy dining out and social events without sacrificing your commitment to a no-carb, no-sugar lifestyle. Remember, it's all about balance and staying focused on your goals while savoring the moment!

Conclusion

Congratulations on completing the No-Carb and No-Sugar Shopping Guide! You've taken an important step toward reclaiming control over your food choices and building a healthier, more intentional lifestyle. This guide was created to empower you with practical tips, strategies, and advice to simplify shopping, dining, and meal planning while staying true to your goals.

Adopting a no-carb, no-sugar lifestyle is more than just a diet—it's a commitment to your well-being. By eliminating hidden sugars and refined carbohydrates, you pave the way for steady energy levels, better focus, and improved overall health. Whether it's navigating grocery store aisles or dining out with confidence, every deliberate choice you make contributes to long-term success.

Remember, the key is to stay prepared and consistent. Meal planning, reading labels, and exploring new ingredients will soon become second nature. Turn shopping into an adventure, discovering nutrient-dense foods that fuel your body and inspire creativity in the kitchen. With each balanced meal you prepare, you're not just nourishing yourself—you're building a foundation for a sustainable lifestyle.

Give yourself grace as you adapt—you don't have to be perfect to make progress. If challenges arise during social events or at restaurants, treat them as learning experiences. Don't hesitate to revisit the tips in this guide, whether you need help mastering food labels, finding budget-friendly options, or whipping up a quick, compliant meal.

FAQs

What are some beginner-friendly tips for planning meals on a no-carb, no-sugar diet?

Start small and plan meals with simple ingredients like grilled proteins (chicken or salmon) and low-carb vegetables (broccoli or zucchini). Choose a few recipes you enjoy and rotate them weekly. Batch cook proteins and prep vegetables in advance to save time during the week. Over time, explore more variety by experimenting with different seasonings and no-carb cooking techniques.

How do I identify hidden sugars and carbs on food labels?

Focus on the ingredients list and avoid items with words like "maltodextrin," "high-fructose corn syrup," or "any ingredient ending in -ose" (e.g., glucose, fructose). Pay attention to "Added Sugars" in the nutrition section and aim for items with 0 added sugars. Lastly, check the total carbs column and calculate net carbs (Total Carbs minus Fiber) if needed.

Can I follow a no-carb, no-sugar diet while dining out?

Yes! Stick to simple dishes like grilled meats, fish, or eggs paired with non-starchy vegetables like spinach or broccoli. Skip carb-heavy sides like rice, bread, or fries, and ask for substitutions like extra greens. Communicate with servers and request sauces or dressings on the side to control hidden sugars.

What are budget-friendly foods to buy on a no-carb, no-sugar diet?

Affordable staples include eggs, canned tuna, seasonal vegetables (like zucchini or kale), and ground beef or chicken. Frozen veggies and proteins can be wallet-friendly and last longer. Purchase cooking oils like olive oil or coconut oil in bulk and opt for conventional produce or meat cuts for additional savings.

What should I look for when shopping for healthy fats?

Choose oils like extra virgin olive oil, coconut oil, or avocado oil for cooking. Nuts like almonds or walnuts provide healthy fats and are great for snacking. Stick to full-fat dairy options like unsweetened yogurt or cheese and avoid products with added sugars or flavorings.

How can I handle social gatherings while sticking to no-carb, no-sugar eating?

Bring your own dish to ensure at least one meal option aligns with your diet. Fill up with protein and low-carb vegetables before indulging in anything else. Focus on connecting with people rather than the food, and consider eating a small meal beforehand in case there are limited options.

How do I prevent boredom with my meals on this diet?

Expand your flavor profiles by using different spices, herbs, and seasonings to keep meals exciting. Experiment with alternatives like zucchini noodles, cauliflower rice, and lettuce wraps. Incorporate global cuisines—like Indian curries (made with coconut milk) or Mexican fajitas (served without tortillas)—to maintain variety without overstepping dietary goals.

References and Helpful Links

Dolson, L. (2024, September 16). Must-Have items for your Low-Carb Grocery List. Verywell Fit. https://www.verywellfit.com/low-carb-grocery-shopping-list-2242501

Msj, J. C. (2020, June 25). The No BS Guide to Healthy Fats. Healthline. https://www.healthline.com/health/food-nutrition/healthy-fats-guidelines

Byrne, C. (2024, October 9). What happens when you stop eating sugar? Health. https://www.health.com/nutrition/what-happens-when-you-stop-eating-sugar#:~:text=Cutting%20out%20or%20limiting%20added,your%20body's%20primary%20energy%20source.

Guevara, J. (2025, January 14). Ultimate No Sugar Diet Food List PDF Guide (2025). JG PILATES. https://jgpilates.com/no-sugar-diet-food-list-pdf/

deMontalk, J. (2023, July 10). How to do a low-sugar grocery shop - Healthy Food Guide. Healthy Food Guide. https://www.healthyfood.com/healthy-shopping/how-to-do-a-low-sugar-grocery-shop/

Nelson, S. (2024, September 13). 20 No Carb Meals and Recipes Packed with Flavor. Chomps. https://chomps.com/blogs/nutrition-sustainability-news/no-carb-recipes#:~:text=Some%20zero%20carb%20meals%20include,fat%20during%20or%20after%20cooking.

Purition UK. (n.d.). Low-carb shopping list for beginners | Blog | Purition. https://www.purition.co.uk/blogs/articles/low-carb-shopping-list-beginners?srsltid=AfmBOooZgCNjJlCY-weMJ1HZpY1IGUDSw_bIr5Wg7s4-eXb0JJleirNr

Printed in Dunstable, United Kingdom